T0193501

THE BOOK OF NORMAN

Autobiography of a Bull

A true story as told by
Bob and Sandy Carroll of Bay Blue Farms

Written by Dr. Tracey Ann Alden, DVM

iUniverse books may be ordered through booksellers or by contacting:

iUniverse
1663 Liberty Drive
Bloomington, IN 47403
www.iuniverse.com
844-349-9409

Because of the dynamic nature of the Internet, any web addresses or links contained
in this book may have changed since publication and may no longer be valid. The views
expressed in this work are solely those of the author and do not necessarily reflect the
views of the publisher, and the publisher hereby disclaims any responsibility for them.

Any people depicted in stock imagery provided by Getty Images are models,
and such images are being used for illustrative purposes only.
Certain stock imagery © Getty Images.

ISBN: 978-1-6632-1209-2 (sc)
ISBN: 978-1-6632-1211-5 (hc)
ISBN: 978-1-6632-1210-8 (e)

Library of Congress Control Number: 2020921299

Print information available on the last page.

iUniverse rev. date: 11/05/2020

This book is presented to you by:
C. A. N. Productions!
Carroll, Alden and Norman that is!

Dedicated to Bob and Sandy Carroll of Bay Blue Farms
Who made the extraordinary life of Norman possible!

INTRODUCTION

Hello, my name is Norman and I live at Bay Blue Farms in Bristow, Oklahoma with some real nice folks, Bob and Sandy Carroll. I am the luckiest Beefmaster steer and once you have heard my story you will see why! I have quite an unusual life for a bovine (that's my family name) and although I do say so myself, I'm pretty *"Bos taurus"* on this farm!

It all started one cold afternoon in the spring of 1998....

A ROUGH BEGINNING

I was born April 8, 1998 on what was supposed to be a fine spring day. Instead, it was so cold my mother's milk could have frozen into ice cream! Mom was supposed to place me gently on the soft ground, but I was such a strapping bull calf that it took two-legged creatures tugging and pulling on my hooves and nose just to get me out!

As far as I was concerned, I was just fine right where I was and the worst was yet to come!

MY FIRST DAY

So, there I was just a bull calf! Most people were disappointed because more heifer calves (those are girl cows) are needed to grow up, produce milk and make babies. So, right off the bat, I felt pretty useless and was not sure what my role in life would be. I did not know what was in store, but I had a sad feeling it wasn't going to be good.

And for what seemed like an eternity I was right!

NOTHING BUT TROUBLE

First of all I had problems with my belly button. It wasn't an "inny" or an "outy" but more like a little balloon sticking out of my tummy! If that wasn't enough my tiny knee swelled up like a baseball! Just when I thought things couldn't get any worse, I was taken away from my mother and all the other animals on the farm that I had come to know in my short life. I was placed in a big box with wheels and taken far, far away.

As the box moved I heard my mother crying
out for me: "MOOOOOOOOOOOOOOO!!!!!"

STRANGE NEW HOME

Once I stepped out of that moving box, strange things really started to happen. More two-legged creatures of all shapes and sizes gathered 'round, poking and prodding as they went. Apparently I was some sort of experiment and I overheard one of them saying there would be an operation to fix the problems I had at birth. I did not like the sound of that, and I liked the looks of the place even less.

Where was the pasture? Where was my mother?

POST-OP BLUES

It seemed as if I were asleep for a long time and when I awoke, I was in another big box, only this time it was not moving. I looked all around to see many rows of boxes with other four-legged creatures sort of like me, but not exactly. They were all making strange sounds and staring at me. The one across from me looked a little like my mom. I cried and cried, but she did not pay any attention to me. Her name was Tanya, and she was a Holstein cow-not my mother! The two next to me were "Samson", a llama, and "Curly", an Angora goat.

Who was I other than a lonely, forgotten bull?

FEEDING TIME

About this time I began to get hungry. Everyone else was eating, but without their mothers. All of a sudden, somebody stuck this rubber thing in my mouth! What was I supposed to do? It felt funny and I tried hard to pull away. But then something sweet and creamy passed over my tongue that reminded me of my mother, so away I drank. This was not so bad! A really nice two-legger was rubbing me and feeding me and saying nice things to me. What's more, my tummy and my knee didn't hurt any longer.

I was starting to feel a little bit better,
but still very lost and confused.

THE NAME

"Norman, that's it!" I heard them say. "Oh, isn't he cute?" "Norman, come here Norman!" they were all saying while pointing at me. I did not know what "Norman" meant, but I assumed it was good since they all looked happy. The one with the rubber milk bottle came by a lot, and I liked that. There were pans in my box with funny-looking straw and gritty sand-like junk, but I didn't know what to do with any of it. I could see Tanya, Samson, and Curly with their faces buried in their pans but that was *NOT* going to work for me!

"I WANT MY BOTTLE", I bawled!

GROWING PAINS

Scream and bawl as I might, my bottle came less and less so I was forced to eat dried hay from a fence and grain from a pail. I guess it's OK if you get hungry enough, but it doesn't compare to Mom's fresh-squeezed! Two-leggers continued to come visit me each day poking and prodding, morning and night. Several times they would walk out to a big shaky square built into the floor then numbers would appear: 125-150-200-275. They seemed happy when the numbers got larger so I went along quietly. Sometimes, I would even go out to buck and sport. Something about that seemed familiar. I was pretty comfortable for the most part, but still didn't seem at home.

Something in my life was missing,
but I didn't know quite what it was.

BARN LIFE

Time passed, and my days were pretty much the same. The two-leggers turned out to be veterinary students who came by all day and were always nice to me. They poured fresh water from a spout, took me for walks outdoors, and one of them brought this little red ball and held it up to my mouth. Believing that everything near my mouth should go inside, I lapped it up with my mighty tongue. "*Wow!* What a treat", I said. Tender, juicy and sweet: I came to know it as an apple. From that day forward, I had at least one apple a day because everyone thought it was so adorable to see a bull eat fruit! Life was good, and I did not want to seem ungrateful, but I continued to feel out of place.

Was this all my life was meant to be, I wondered?

NORMAN'S FATE

"What is a bull *really* supposed to do?" I'd wonder, and one of the veterinary students knew something had to be done with me soon. I began to hear talk of what was to become of me, some of which did not sound too appealing! I heard some folks make a meal out of creatures like me. Other folks ride on horses and tie ropes around our legs. In some parts of the world people actually want to see how mad they can make a bull by chasing him around a ring waving a big red cape. Many bulls just get sent out to pasture to wait for a willing cow to have little ones just like me. Hmmm.....

After many weeks of discussion,
my fate was finally decided.

THE JOURNEY HOME

Outfitted in a scarf made especially for bulls, I was placed into another moving box. Tears streamed down my face, as the journey was bittersweet; I was sad to leave the nice people at the school, but overjoyed to hear familiar voices. Could I be going back to the place I left so long ago? We traveled down a long road with lots of bumps as an eternity seemed to pass. Through the dust in my eyes, I could see a big white fence surrounding a barn, barking dogs, baying horses, and many other four-legged creatures just like me curious to see the new arrival.

It was true! I was home and my dreams had been fulfilled!

LIFE ON THE FARM

Life could not have been better! I met my relatives, made new friends, and was treated daily to apples from my very own tree! With time I moved on to ripe juicy pears and tasty pellets. People, horses, dogs, cows, and an occasional cat surrounded my world. My days were filled with friendly visitors, funny holiday costumes, and photo shoots which included my cinematographic debut! My favorite duty was baby sitting all the newborn calves on the farm. Even though none of them belonged to me, I loved them just the same.

My life now had purpose:
I couldn't be more happy and content!

MY PURPOSE IN LIFE

I now know what this young bull calf was meant to do! My days are blessed with friends, laughter love, sunshine and lots of good food! I have the *BEST* life ever: a happy ending to this story, and a new beginning for more wonderful things to come.

I hope you'll come visit me and let me share more of my happy tales. So long for now!

Love,
Norman

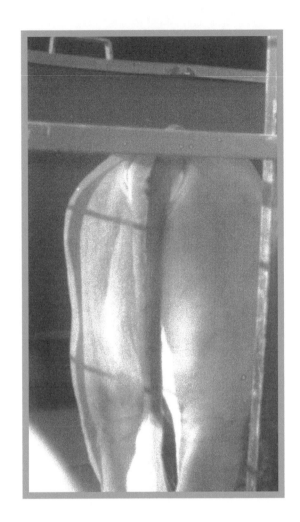

THE END

A TRIBUTE

To those who made my story come to life!

What can I say about my human mom and dad, **Bob and Sandy**? They've given me a wonderful life and I love them dearly. Bob has his hands full with ranching and many creative talents while Sandy is a medical doctor in Tulsa, Oklahoma. They are caring, giving people who love animals and provide an excellent home for all that come their way.

I first met **Dr. Tracey Alden** at Oklahoma State University in the summer of 1998. If it hadn't been for her I might have ended up being served at the annual BBQ! All the doctors and students at OSU wanted to see me get a good home and thanks to so much effort on everyone's part that's just what I did. Tracey is a veterinarian in Edmond, Oklahoma and continues to visit me regularly, always hollering my name and toting an apple in one hand and a pear in the other.

Last but certainly not least, I must pay homage to the ones that gave me life: my biological father and mother, **Spot and Chunky**. It all began with your love for each other and I am the legacy you created. I hope I always make you proud. Thanks for giving me life- I love you both! Even though mom and dad are no longer with me, **Grandma**, who was born in 1985 spends her senior days in the pasture with me!

Printed in the United States
By Bookmasters